Kid's Box

Box

New Generation

Caroline Nixon &
Michael Tomlinson

Student's Book
with eBook
American English

2

CAMBRIDGE

Language summary

		Key vocabulary	**Key language**	**Sounds and spelling**
1	**Hi again!** page 4	**Character names:** Mr. Star, Mrs. Star, Sally, Scott, Suzy, Grandma Star, Grandpa Star, Marie, Maskman, Monty, Trevor **Numbers:** 1–10 **The alphabet** **Colors:** red, yellow, pink, green, orange, blue, purple, brown, black, white, gray	**Greetings:** Hi. We're the Star family. Who's he/she? This is my brother, Scott. He's seven. And this is my sister, Suzy. She's four. **Prepositions:** in, on, under	**Consonant sound:** *wh* (<u>wh</u>ale)
2	**Back to school** page 10	**School:** bookcase, board, cupboard, computer, desk, ruler, teacher, TV, whiteboard **Character names:** Alex, Robert, Eva **Numbers:** 11–20	How many (books) are there? There's / There isn't a (whiteboard). There are / aren't (11 desks). Is there (a ruler) on the (desk)? Yes, there is. / No, there isn't. Are there (19 pens) on the (desk)? Yes, there are. / No, there aren't.	**Long vowel sound:** *ee* (b<u>ee</u>)

Marie's math: What do we use in our math class?   page 16   **Trevor's values:** Be polite   page 17

		Key vocabulary	**Key language**	**Sounds and spelling**
3	**Playtime!** page 18	**Toys:** alien, camera, board game, kite, truck, robot, tablet, watch, teddy bear	this, that, these, those Whose is it? / Whose (kite) is this? It's Sally's. Whose (shoes) are these? They're Sheila's.	**Long vowel sound:** *i–e* (k<u>i</u>t<u>e</u>)
4	**At home** page 24	**Furniture:** clock, lamp, rug, mirror, phone, couch	mine / yours / his / hers Which shoes are (Scott's / Sally's)? The (gray) ones are (his/hers).	**Consonant sound:** *–se* (no<u>se</u>)

Marie's art: What can you do with origami?   page 30   **Trevor's values:** Reuse and recycle   page 31

Review: units 1, 2, 3, and 4   page 32

		Key vocabulary	**Key language**	**Sounds and spelling**
5	**Meet my family** page 34	**Family:** baby, cousin, mom, dad, grandma, grandpa **Character names:** Tony, Alice, Nick, Kim, Hugo, Lucy, May, Robert, Sam, Frank	Robert's hitting the ball. He isn't walking. What's Grandpa doing? **Verb + -ing spellings:** catching, cleaning, flying, getting, hitting, jumping, kicking, running, sitting, sleeping, talking, throwing	**Consonant sound:** *c, ck,* and *k* (<u>c</u>at, clo<u>ck</u>, loo<u>k</u>)
6	**Dinnertime** page 40	**Food:** bread, chicken, fries, eggs, juice, milk, rice, water	Can I have an (egg) / some (bread), please? Here you are.	**Consonant sound:** *ch* (<u>ch</u>icken)

Marie's science: Where does food come from?   page 46   **Trevor's values:** Eat good food   page 47

1 Hi again!

1 🎧 2-3 **Listen and point. Listen and repeat.**

What's your name?
How old are you?

Mrs. Star

Sally

Grandma Star

Mr. Star

Scott

Suzy

Grandpa Star

2 **Point and say.**

Who's she?

She's Sally.

Vocabulary presentation 1: character names | **Language presentation 1:** greetings *Hi. Who's he/she?*

Hi, I'm Trevor. Look at number four. Who's he?

2 Ask and answer.

Look at number three. Who's she?

Sally.

1 🎵🎧 5-6 **Listen, point, and repeat. Say the chant.**

Aa

Bb

Cc Dd Ee Ff Gg Hh

Ii Jj Kk Ll Mm

Nn Oo Pp Qq

Rr Ss Tt

Uu Vv Ww

Xx Yy

Zz

2 **Play and say.**

Hello. I'm gray. Which letters make my sound?

a, h, j, k

Vocabulary presentation and practice 3: the alphabet and colors

1 Ask and answer. | Can you spell "purple"? | P-u-r-p-l-e. | **1**

2 Put the colors in order. Write numbers.

Black, blue, brown ...

gray

pink ☐

green ☐

☐

orange

brown ☐

☐

white

red

blue

☐

☐

purple

☐

yellow ☐

black [1]

3 Spell and guess. | C-a-t. | Cat! |

1 🎧 7 ▶ **Watch and say.**

Where's the white whale?
Next to the wheel!

2 **Ask and answer.**

Where's the white whale?

The white whale is on the wheel.

Write it with me!

___ ale

1 🎧 8 ▶ Watch the video.

2 🎧 9 Listen and say the number.

2 Back to school

board
teacher
cupboard
bookcase
ruler
desk

2 **Play and say.** What color is the ruler? It's brown.

 **Listen and point. Say the chant.**

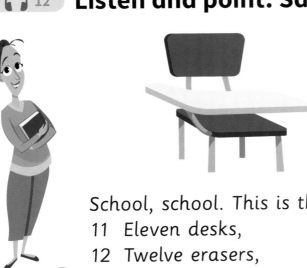

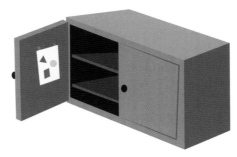

School, school. This is the Numbers School.
11 Eleven desks,
12 Twelve erasers,
13 Thirteen rulers,
14 Fourteen cupboards,
15 Fifteen classrooms,
16 Sixteen teachers,
17 Seventeen pens,
18 Eighteen boards,
19 Nineteen pencils,
20 Twenty tables.
School, school. This is the Numbers School.

 Ask and answer.

(How many desks are there?) (Eleven.)

This is my classroom. How many desks are there? There are a lot of desks. That's my desk next to the bookcase. There's a long pink ruler on it. There are a lot of books in the bookcase. There's a big whiteboard on the wall. There's a computer, but there isn't a TV.

2 **Play and say.**

There are nineteen chairs.

No.

There are pencils in the classroom, yes there are.
There's a cupboard on the pencils, yes there is.
There's a ruler on the cupboard.
There's a bookcase on the ruler.
There's a teacher on the bookcase, yes there is ...

2 **Ask and answer.**

Where's the cupboard?   On the pencils.

Language practice 2: *There's a ruler on the cupboard.*   13

1 🎧 17 ▶ **Watch and say.**

How many bees can you see?
Seventeen bees in the tree!

2 **Ask and answer.** How many … are there? There are …

Write it with me!

 b _ _ _

1 🎧 18 ▶ Watch the video.

1 OK, everybody. This backpack is for school. Let's look.

OK, Marie!

2 Hmm. Is there a ruler?

Yes, there is. It's a "Maskman" ruler.

3 Look, Marie. Here's an eraser.

Good! Can you put it in the backpack, please, Monty?

4 Now there's an eraser in the backpack, Marie.

Good! Thank you, Monty.

5 Now, how many pencils are there?

There are 9, 10, 11 pencils.

6 11 pencils! Where's the pencil? Trevor!

Sorry. Here you are. Pencils are my favorite food.

2 🎧 19 Listen and say "yes" or "no."

Story: unit language in context

Marie's math

What do we use in our math class?

1 ▶ **Watch and answer.**

2 🎧 20 **Listen and number.**

a  b  c  d

3 **Look, ask, and answer.**

Is there a pen in Ben's pencil case?

Yes, there are four pens.

Ben <u>Bar chart</u>

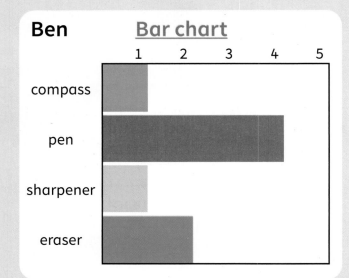

	1	2	3	4	5
compass					
pen					
sharpener					
eraser					

Eva <u>Pictogram</u>

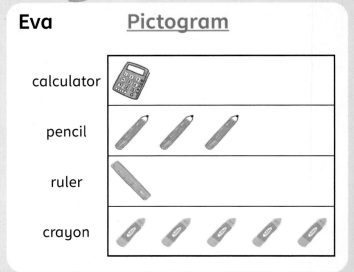

calculator	
pencil	
ruler	
crayon	

The first calculator is 190 years old. This is a part of it!

Fact

Project

Design a bar chart or pictogram

Trevor's values

Be polite

1 🎧 21 **Listen and say the number.**

2 **Act it out.**

3 **Play and say.**   Picture four!   I can share my pencils.

3 Playtime!

1 🎧 22-23 **Listen and point. Listen and repeat.**

truck

kite

Trucks

Kites

Watches

watch

camera

Cameras

Board ga...

Robots

alien

board games

robot

Teddy bears

teddy bear

tablet

2 **Play and say.**

C-a-m-e-r-a!

That's camera!

Vocabulary presentation: toys

1 🎧 24 **Listen and say the number.**

These are dolls. | 19. | This is a robot. | 17.

2 🎧 25 **Listen and say "yes" or "no."**

 **Listen and point. Listen and repeat.**

 Ask and answer. Whose is this? It's Suzy's.

Language practice 1: *this / these* | Language presentation 2: *Whose is it / (kite) is this? It's Sally's.*

1 🎵🎧 28-29 ▶ Listen and sing. Do karaoke.

Whose jacket is this?
What? That black jacket?
Yes, this black jacket.
Whose jacket is this?
It's John's.
Oh!

Whose shoes are these?
What? Those blue shoes?
Yes, these blue shoes.
Whose shoes are these?
They're Sheila's.
Oh!

Whose skirt is this?
What? That purple skirt?
Yes, this purple skirt.
Whose skirt is this?
It's Sue's.
Oh!

Whose pants are these?
What? Those brown pants?
Yes, these brown pants.
Whose pants are these?
They're Tom's.
Oh!

 Ask and answer.

Whose pants are these?   They're Tom's.

monty's sounds and spelling

1 🎧 30 ▶ **Watch and say.**

Hide the five kites and ride the white bike!

2 **Play and say.**

> Which kite is my kite?

> Is it the blue and red kite?

Write it with me!

k _ t _

 **Watch the video.**

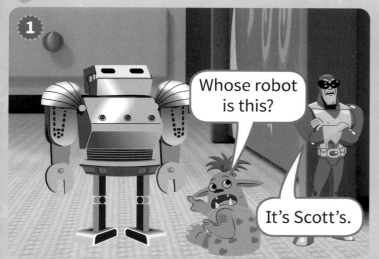

 Act out the story.

4 At home

1 🎧 32–33 **Listen and point. Listen and repeat.**

mirror

rug

clock

couch

phone

lamp

2 **Ask and answer.**

What color's the clock in the kitchen?   It's orange.

24   **Vocabulary presentation:** furniture

1  34 Listen and point. Say the chant.

There's a mirror in the bathroom
And a phone in the hallway.
A couch in the living room,
A clock on the wall.
There's a lamp on the table
And a rug next to the bed.
There's a boat in the bathtub,
And the boat is red.

2  35 Listen and correct.

There's a girl sitting on the couch.

There's a boy sitting on the couch.

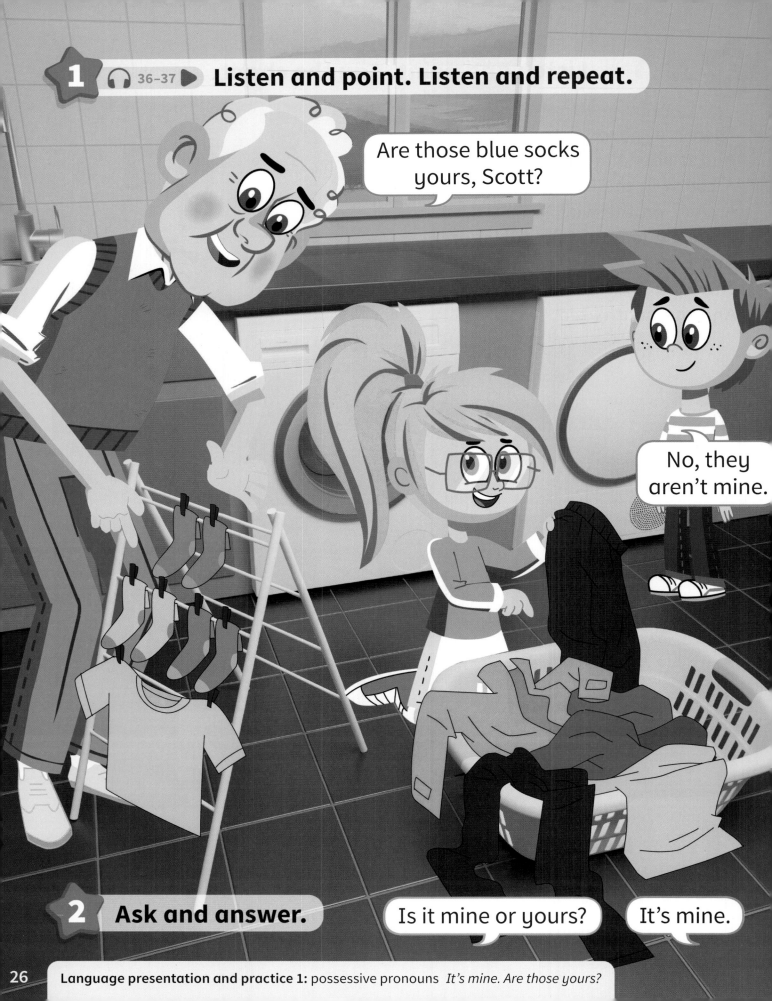

Language presentation and practice 1: possessive pronouns *It's mine. Are those yours?*

Look at this!
Look at this!

Whose shoes are these?
Sally! Are they yours?
No, they aren't mine!

Hmm. Which shoes are Scott's?
Which, which, which, which?
Which shoes are Scott's?
The gray ones are his.

Hmm. Which shoes are Suzy's?
Which, which, which, which?
Which shoes are Suzy's?
The red ones are hers.

So! Whose shoes are those?
Whose, whose, whose, whose?
Whose shoes are those?
Those are Grandpa's.
Grandpa's?

GRANDPA!

2 **Ask and answer.**

Which backpack is yours? The red one's mine.

Language presentation and practice 2: *Which shoes are Scott's / Sally's? The gray ones are his/hers.*   27

monty's sounds and spelling

1 🎧 40 ▶ **Watch and say.**

*Who**s**e no**s**es are tho**s**e? Look and choo**s**e!*

2 **Ask and answer.**

Whose nose is this?

It's Scott's.

11

12

13

14

15

16

17

18

Write it with me!

no ___ ___

1  41 ▶ Watch the video.

1 Let's play hide and seek.

Trevor, close your eyes and count to 20.

2 … 15, 16, 17, 18, 19, 20. I'm coming.

3 Where are they? Whose tail is that? Ha ha! I can see you, Monty. You're under the armchair.

OK. Good job, Trevor.

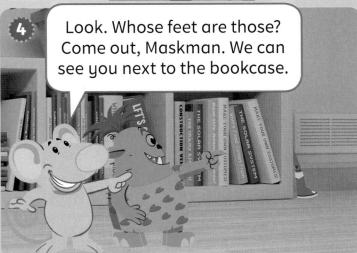

4 Look. Whose feet are those? Come out, Maskman. We can see you next to the bookcase.

5 Now, where's Marie?

Marie's in the cupboard. Look! That's her hair.

6 Eeeek! What's that?

I win!

It's a toy horse.

2  42 Listen and say the number.

Marie's art

What can you do with origami?

 Watch and answer.

 Match and say.

Number 1. Star!

box ☐ bird ☐ heart ☐ star 1 flower ☐

3 🎧 43 **Listen and write.**

~~bird~~ box flower heart star

 Clara
 Chen
 Flora
 Tina
 Adam

bird

Fact
The world record for the number of origami elephants is 78,564!

Project

Make origami games.

30 Marie's art | 🛡 creative thinking

Trevor's values

Reuse and recycle

1 🎧 44 **Listen and say the number.**

1

2

3

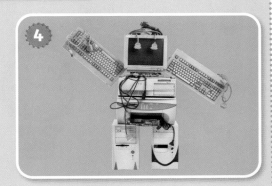
4

2 **Ask and answer.**

What's this?

It's an elephant.

What's it made from?

It's made from bottles.

3 **What do you reuse at home?**

I reuse … at home.

paper

bottles

plastic bags

1 🎧 45 **Listen and say the number.**

11 12 13 14 15

16 17 18 19 20

2 **Look and say.**

In picture one there's a blue rug on the floor, but in picture two there's a purple rug on the floor.

1 2

1 Play the game. Ask and answer.

What number is this?   **19.**

What's this?

What number is this?
16

What number is this?
15

What are these?

What's this?

What room is this?

What number is this?
12

What color is the couch?

What are these?

What number is this?
19

What's this?

What number is this?
20

What's this?

What are these?

What number is this?
17

What's this?

What number is this?
14

What's this?
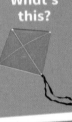

What number is this?
11

What's this?

Where are the books?

What's this?

What number is this?
13

What room is this?

What are these?

Finish

What number is this?
15

What's this?

What are these?

What number is this?
18

Start

5 Meet my family

1 🎧 46–47 **Listen and point. Listen and repeat.**

dad

mom

grandpa

cousi

grandma

baby

2 Play and say.

Spell "baby," please.   B-a-b-y.

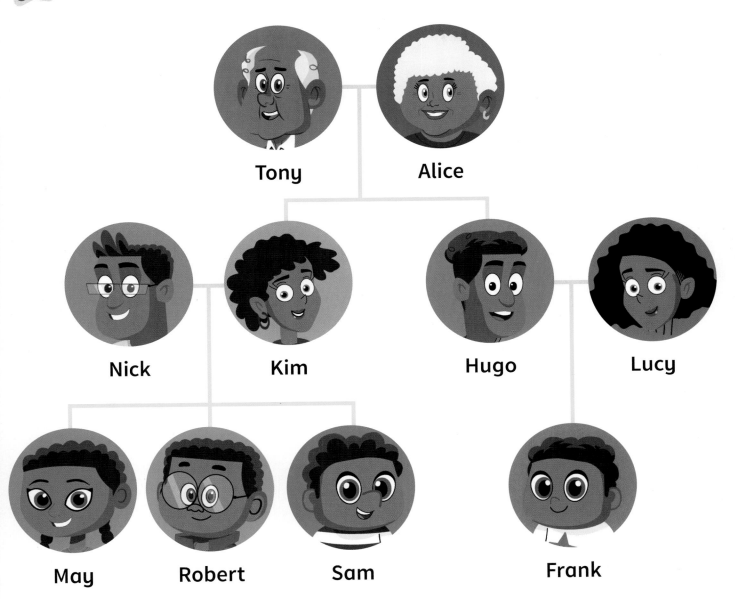

Tony   Alice

Nick   Kim   Hugo   Lucy

May   Robert   Sam   Frank

2 **Look and say.**

He's Robert's father.   Nick.

3 **Play and say "yes" or "no."**

Kim is Hugo's sister.   Yes.

1 🎧 49 ▶ Listen and say the number.

2 Make sentences. Use the words in the box.

The dog's getting the ball.

getting   throwing   catching   flying   talking   jumping
sitting   hitting   cleaning   running   kicking   sleeping

Language presentation and practice 1: present continuous *Robert's hitting the ball.*

1  50–51 ▶ Listen and sing. Do karaoke.

My grandpa isn't walking,
He's flying my favorite kite.
My grandma's cleaning the table,
It's beautiful and white.

My father's playing baseball,
He can catch, and he can hit.
My cousin has the ball now,
And now he's throwing it.

My baby sister's sleeping,
She is very small.
My brother isn't jumping,
He's kicking his soccer ball.
Hey!

My grandpa isn't walking,
He's flying my favorite kite.
My grandma's cleaning the table,
It's beautiful and white.
My mother's sitting reading,
Her book is big and gray.
And me? I'm very happy,
I can run and play …

2 Ask and answer.

What's Grandpa doing?   He's flying a kite.

Monty's sounds and spelling

1  52 ▶ **Watch and say.**

Look, crocodile! A cat in a coat is taking your cup!

2 **Look and choose. Ask and answer.**

What's the cat doing?

The cat's cleaning a clock.

(cow) (cat) (snake) (crocodile) (duck) (monkey)

Write it with me!
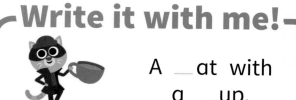
A __ at with
a __ up.

Sounds and spelling: *c, ck,* and *k*

1 🎧 53 ▶ Watch the video.

2 🎧 54 Listen and say the number.

6 Dinnertime

1 🎧 55–56 **Listen and point. Listen and repeat.**

rice

milk

juice

water

bread

Cake Mix

fries

eggs

chicken

2 **Ask and answer.**

What can you see in the kitchen?

I can see bread.

Vocabulary presentation: food

1 🎵🎧 57–58 ▶ Listen and sing. Do karaoke.

It's morning, it's morning.
We're having breakfast with our mom.
Bread and milk, bread and milk.
It's morning, it's morning.

It's lunchtime, it's lunchtime.
We're having lunch with our friends.
Eggs and fries, eggs and fries.
It's lunchtime, it's lunchtime.

It's afternoon, it's afternoon.
We're having a snack in the backyard.
Chocolate cake, chocolate cake.
We're having a snack in the afternoon.

It's evening, it's evening.
We're having dinner with Mom and Dad.
Chicken and rice, chicken and rice.
It's evening, it's evening …

2 Point, ask, and answer.

What's this?   It's chocolate cake.   What are these?   They're fries.

Vocabulary practice: food   41

59–60 ▶ **Listen and answer. Listen and repeat.**

Can I have some brown bread, please?

Here you are.

2 **Act it out.**

Language presentation: polite requests *Can I have some bread, please? Here you are.*

Play bingo.

 Read and answer.

Hi. My name's Alex. I'm Scott's friend. It's lunchtime, and I'm having 🐟 and 🍟 for lunch. 🐟 isn't my favorite lunch. My favorite lunch is 🍖. In the morning, my favorite breakfast is 🍎🍌 and 🥛🥛, and my favorite dinner is 🍗 and 🍚.

1 What's his favorite breakfast?
2 What's his favorite lunch?
3 What's his favorite dinner?

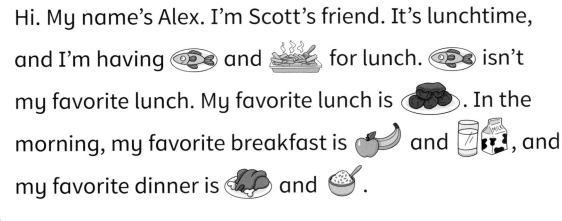

Monty's sounds and spelling

1 🎧 61 ▶ **Watch and say.**

The **ch**icken's lun**ch** is **ch**eese, fries, and **ch**ocolate!

2 **Choose and draw. Ask and answer.**

What's for lunch?

On my plate there's some fish and fries and water – that's my lunch!

Write it with me!

_ _ icken

1 🎧 62 ▶ Watch the video.

1. I'm having tomatoes and carrots.

2. Can I have some apple juice, please?

3. Here you are.

Is there any chocolate cake?

4. No, there isn't, but there's some chocolate ice cream.

5. Is this orange juice yours, Monty?

No, it isn't mine. It's Marie's.

6. What are you eating, Trevor? Is it chicken?

Um, no. It isn't chicken. It's a long brown pencil!

Oh, Trevor!

2 🎧 63 Listen and say "yes" or "no."

Story: unit language in context

Marie's science

Where does food come from?

 Watch and answer.

 Look and say.

> Meat is from animals.

> Carrots are from plants.

 Look, read, and complete.

vegetables   cows   meat   milk   plants   yogurt

> My favorite food is _____ .
> It comes from the _____ of
> animals, like _____ and sheep.

Nick

Maya

> My favorite food is _____ . They
> come from _____ . My family is
> vegetarian. We don't eat _____ .

> There are a lot of different ice cream flavors: cheese ice cream, potato ice cream, and fish ice cream!

Fact

Project

Design a food poster.

Trevor's values

Eat good food

1 🎧 64 **Listen and say the number.**

Breakfast

Lunch

Dinner

2 **Ask and answer.**

What's number one?

It's a bad breakfast.

What's number four?

It's a good lunch.

7 On the farm

1 🎧 65–66 **Listen and point. Listen and repeat.**

donkey

sheep

cow

spider

goat

duck

lizard

frog

Entrance

2 Ask and answer.

What's this?

It's a cow. Moo!

48

Vocabulary presentation: animals

1  **Listen and sing. Do karaoke.**

Cows in the kitchen, moo moo moo,
Cows in the kitchen.
There are cows in the kitchen, moo moo moo.
What can we do, John Farmer?

Sheep in the bedroom, baa baa baa ...

Ducks on the armchair, quack quack quack ...

Frogs in the bathroom, croak croak croak ...

Chickens in the cupboard, cluck cluck cluck ...

2 **Look, ask, and answer.**

Where's the donkey?   It's in the garden.

Vocabulary practice: animals   49

🎧 69–70 ▶ **Listen and answer. Listen and repeat.**

2 Act it out.

Language presentation: agreeing and disagreeing *I love horses. So do I. I don't.*

 **Listen and point. Say the chant.**

I love watermelon.	So do I.
I love pineapple.	So do I.
I love bananas.	So do I.
I love oranges.	So do I.
I love mangoes.	So do I.
I love coconuts.	So do I.
I love lemon and lime.	Hmm. So do I.
I love onions.	I don't. Goodbye.

2 Read and choose. Say and play.

(I like cats.) (So do I.) (I like spiders.) (I don't.)

1 I like

3 I like

2 I love

4 I love

Language practice: agreeing and disagreeing *I love watermelon. So do I. I don't.* 51

monty's sounds and spelling

1 🎧 72 ▶ **Watch and say.**

A **sl**ow **sn**ail, a **sc**ary **sn**ake, and a **sp**eedy **sp**ider!

Play and say.

They're brown, and they have long legs.

Spiders!

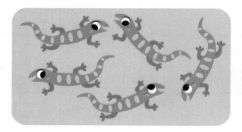

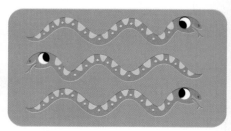

Write it with me!

A ____ake and
a ____ider!

1 🎧 73 ▶ Watch the video.

1 Trevor! Pssst! Are you sleeping?

Yes, I am.

2 Trevor! Maskman! Can you be quiet, please? I'm trying to sleep!

3 I can't sleep.

Well, count sheep, Maskman.

4 11, 12, 13 … Oh, no! My sheep aren't sleeping. They're jumping! I can't sleep.

We can't sleep now!

5 OK, let's talk about farms. Farm dogs can get sheep. Farm cats can catch mice. And we get milk from cows.

Yes, yes, I know. Maskman!

6 What are you doing, Maskman?

I'm sleeping, Marie. Goodnight.

 2 Act out the story.

Story: unit language in context   53

8 ★ My town

park

apartment

Pete's Pets

Flora's Flowers

Smart Clothes

TOYS 4 U

hospital

Good Food Café

store

Small Feet Shoes

café

Good Food Café

street

2 **Ask and answer.**

Spell "café," please.   C-a-f-e.

Read and answer.

1 Where's the woman with the dog?
2 How many pineapples are there?
3 How many dogs are there?
4 Where's the boy with the kite?
5 What color are the boots in the shoe store?
6 Where are the lemons?
7 What color's the bus?

Ask, count, and answer.

How many skateboards are there?   There are two skateboards.

babies   cars   children   coconuts   lemons   men
pineapples   planes   skateboards   trains   women

Vocabulary practice: places and plural nouns   55

Language presentation: prepositions *behind*, *between*, *in front of*

 **Listen and sing. Do karaoke.**

> Put two books on the table …
> Put a pencil between the books …
> Put a pencil behind your head …
> Put a book in front of your nose …
> Put a book under your chair …
> Put a pencil behind your ear …
> Put two books on your head …
> Put them all back on the table,
> And now, now, sit down.

2 Read and say. Write.

There's a black book _next to_ the armchair. There's a brown book _____ the dog, and there's a purple book _____ the yellow bag. There's an orange book the couch and the table.

Monty's sounds and spelling

1 🎧 79 ▶ **Watch and say.**

**They're playing in the park.
Hippo is hopping! Panda is jumping!**

2 **Ask and answer.** Where's the panda? Next to the snake.

Write it with me!

hi____o and
____anda

Sounds and spelling: *p* and *pp*

1 🎧 80 ▶ **Watch the video.**

2 🎧 81 **Listen and say the number.**

Marie's geography

Where do we live?

1 ▶ **Watch and answer.**

2 **Read and match. Write.**

1 This is my town. It isn't small, and it isn't very big. It has stores, a supermarket, and a movie theater. It's next to the ocean.

2 This is my town. It's small. It has two stores, a bakery, and a little library.

3 This is my city! It's very big. It's busy with people, cars, and buses every day.

a

b

c

3 **Find and write the words. Ask and answer.**

> bakery   movie theater   ~~library~~   playground   school

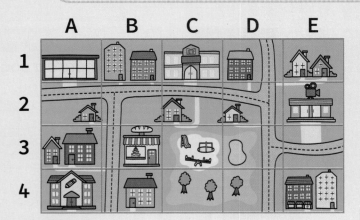

A   B   C   D   E
1
2
3
4

1 C1 = *library*
2 B3 = _____
3 C3 = _____
4 E2 = _____
5 A4 = _____

This is a floating town in Thailand. All the people live on boats!

Fact

Project

Make a town plan and fact file.

Trevor's values

Be responsible in your town

1 🎧 82 **Listen and say the number.**

2 **Look and say with a friend.**

> We can recycle bottles.

> Picture four.

1 🎧 83 Listen and say the letter.

a

b

c

d

e

f

2 Read and answer.

Leo and Ivan are on the farm today.

They're looking at the . Next to it

there are three . They're eating .

A is . Ivan's very .

1 Where is Leo?

2 What are they looking at?

3 How many ducks are there?

4 What's the frog doing?

Play the game. Answer the question.

Where's the star?   It's in front of the hospital.

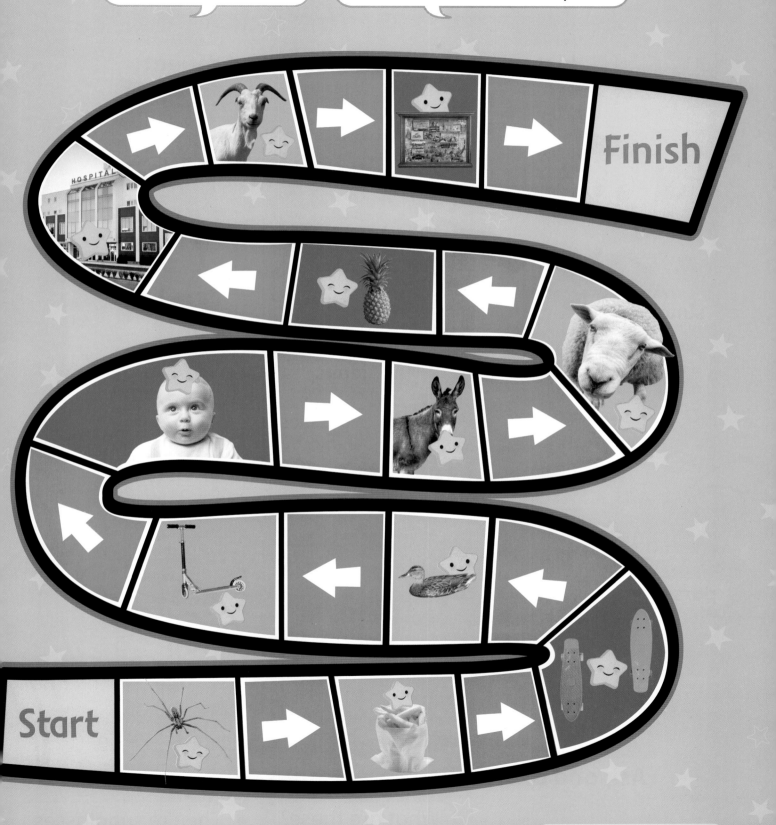

9 Our clothes

1 🎧 84-85 **Listen and answer. Listen and repeat.**

sunglasses

shirt

jeans

glasses

hat

purse

dress

2 **Ask and answer.**

What are these?   They're sunglasses.

64   Vocabulary presentation: clothes

1  86–87 Say the chant. Listen and correct.

> There's a big box with toys.

> No, there's a big box with clothes.

Purses, glasses,
Jackets, and shirts.
T-shirts, pants,
Dresses, and skirts.
Hats, jeans,
Shoes, and socks.
Put them on,
They're in the box.

2 Read and say "yes" or "no."

1 Two girls are wearing long pink dresses. No.

2 Three boys are wearing hats.

3 Two girls are wearing glasses.

4 Four boys are wearing sunglasses.

5 Two girls are wearing skirts.

1 🎧 88–89 ▶ Listen and point. Listen and repeat.

I have a big car.
Do you have a car, Trevor?

No, I don't.

2 Ask and answer.

Does Maskman have a blue car?

Yes, he does.

Language presentation 2: *have* questions and answers *Do you have a big car? Yes, I do. / No, I don't.*

 Listen and sing. Do karaoke.

I have a big yard,
I have a big house.
I have a good friend,
A small toy mouse.
I have you, Monty.
I have you.

Oh, Marie!

I have a black mask
And a big blue car.
I have black glasses,
I'm the Maskman star,
And I have you, Monty.
I have you.

Oh, Maskman!

I don't have
Superhero clothes.
I have purple hair
And a big green nose,
And I have you, Monty.
I have you.

Oh, Trevor!

I have you, Monty.
I have you.

 Ask and answer.

Do you have a yard?   Yes, I do.

Language practice 2: *have* affirmative, negative, questions, and answers   67

Monty's sounds and spelling

1 🎧 92 ▶ **Watch and say.**

A jellyfish in a jacket juggling jugs and juice!

2 **Ask your friend.**

Do you have sunglasses and a yellow jacket in your picture?

No.

1

2

3

4

Write it with me!

_ ellyfish

9

1 🎧 93 ▶ Watch the video.

2 🎧 94 Listen and say the number.

10 Our hobbies

skateboarding

badminton

painting

Ping-Pong

field hockey

basketball

baseball

2 Play and say.

P-a-i-n-t-i-n-g! Painting!

Vocabulary presentation: hobbies

1 🎧 97 **Listen and match. Say the hobby.**

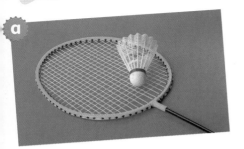
a

b

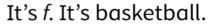
It's *f*. It's basketball.

c

d

e

f

2 **Read and answer.**

These children are playing soccer. This sport has two names: soccer and football. On a soccer team, there are ten players who can run and kick the ball, and one player who can kick and catch the ball. This player is the goalkeeper. Can you see the goalkeeper in this picture? She's wearing an orange T-shirt, black shorts, and yellow shoes.

1 The children are playing
  a badminton
  b basketball
  c football.

2 Eleven players can
  a kick the ball
  b catch the ball
  c bounce the ball.

3 One player can
  a run
  b hit the ball
  c catch the ball.

 **1** 🎧 98 ▶ **Listen and say the number.**

Number three.

1

Name: Grandpa Star
Likes: fishing and badminton
Dislikes: cleaning his shoes

2

Name: Robert
Likes: swimming and soccer
Dislikes: Ping-Pong

3

Name: Mr. Star
Likes: the guitar and cooking
Dislikes: horses

4

Name: Grandma Star
Likes: painting and driving
Dislikes: gardening

5

Name: Eva
Likes: bikes and pictures
Dislikes: TV

6

Name: Alex
Likes: badminton and the piano
Dislikes: baseball

7

Name: Scott
Likes: basketball and field hockey
Dislikes: cleaning his room

8

Name: Mrs. Star
Likes: horses and reading
Dislikes: cooking

9
Name: Suzy
Likes: singing and drawing
Dislikes: soccer

10

Name: Sally
Likes: the piano and reading
Dislikes: playing sports

 2 **Say and play.**

She likes horses and reading, but she doesn't like cooking.

Mrs. Star.

Language presentation and practice 1: *I love / like / don't like singing. She likes / doesn't like cooking.*

1  Listen and sing. Do karaoke.

I ♥♥ fishing,
I ♥♥ flying kites.
I ♥ taking pictures,
I ♥ riding bikes.
I ♥♥ fishing!
Bedum … bedoo.

I ♥♥ swimming,
Playing field hockey, too.
And I ♥♥ painting
With the color blue.
I ♥♥ swimming!
Bedum … bedoo.

I ✗ driving
Or flying in a plane.
I ✗ cleaning shoes.
I ✗ running for a train!
Bedum … bedoo.

I ✗ cooking
Or playing the guitar.
I ✗ badminton
Or cleaning my dad's car.
I ✗ it!
Bedum … bedoo. Yeh!

2 Ask and answer.

Does Scott like painting?

Yes, he does.

Monty's sounds and spelling

1 🎧 101 ▶ **Watch and say.**

*The wh**a**le and the sn**ai**l are pl**ay**ing b**a**seball tod**ay**.*

2 **Choose, draw, and say.** (♥ ✓ ✗) The whale loves …

Write it with me!

The sn ___ l's pl ___ ing b ___ s ___ ball.

74 **Sounds and spelling:** *a–e, ai,* and *ay*

1  102 ▶ **Watch the video.**

2 103 **Listen and say "yes" or "no."**

Story: unit language in context   75

Marie's sports

What sports can we do in summer and winter?

1 ▶ **Watch and answer.**

2 **Read and match.**

1 We can go hiking in the mountains in summer.

2 I really like skiing when it snows.

3 Snowboarding is very popular in winter.

4 We like sailing in summer.

5 I love surfing on big waves! I'm not scared!

6 I love snorkeling in the warm water.

a

b

c

d

e

f  1

3 **What summer and winter sports do you like to do?**

Dogs like surfing, too! In the USA, there's a surfing competition for dogs every September.

Fact

Project

Do a hobbies survey.

Trevor's values

Follow the rules

1 🎧 104 **Listen and say the number.**

2 **Look and say with a friend.**

You can kick the ball.

Soccer.

11 My birthday

1 🎧 105–106 **Listen and answer. Listen and repeat.**

Happy Birthday Scott

sausages

salad

watermelon

cake

pie

lemonade

oranges

2 **Play and say.**

How many burgers are there?

There are two.

1  107 Listen and point. Say the chant.

Look at them,
Five young men.
Look at him,
He can swim.
Look at her
In her new skirt.
Look at you
And your nice clean shoe.
Look at us
On a big red bus.
Look at me,
I'm under a tree.

2 Read and write.

Birthday party

It's my birthday ___party___ this afternoon. Mom and Dad are doing things in the house, and I'm helping them. Dad's in the kitchen. He's making a big 1 _____ for us. Mom's in the living room. She's putting a salad on the 2 _____ next to a big, green and red 3 _____. There are a lot of burgers and 4 _____. We have 5 _____ to drink.

Example

party

sausages

table

hall

cake

watermelon

lemonade

bed

Language presentation 2: *Would you like a burger or a sausage? I'd like a burger, please. Yes, I'd love one / some.*

1  110–111 ▶ **Listen and sing. Do karaoke.**

11

I'd like a great big chocolate cake,
And I'd like one for me.
I'd like a nice long sausage,
And I'd like one for me.

I'd like a burger and some fries,
And I'd like some for me.
I'd like a drink of lemonade,
And I'd like some for me.

I'd like colored pencils, …
I'd like a box of colored pencils.

Don't give any to me!

2 **Ask and answer.**

(Would you like a burger?)   (Yes, please.)   (No, thank you.)

monty's sounds and spelling

1 🎧 112 ▶ **Watch and say.**

Happy birthday, purple bird!
Let's eat a burger at the circus!

2 **Say and play.** The girl has some birthday cake. Picture 3!

Write it with me!

p _ _ _ ple b _ _ _ d

1  113 ▶ Watch the video.

1 It's Marie's birthday today.

Let's have a party for Marie! Let's make her a pencil cake.

No, Trevor. Marie would like a lemon cake.

2 Let's have burgers and fries to eat.

No, Maskman. It isn't your birthday.

3 Let's make the cake now!

4 Ssh. Marie's coming!

Now we can't make her a cake.

5 Happy birthday, Marie!

6 Thanks, boys! Would you like to come to the café with me?

Can I have some pencil cake, please?

2 Act out the story.

Story: unit language in context 83

12 On vacation!

School

1 🎧 114–115 **Listen and point. Listen and repeat.**

sun

mountain

shell

ocean

sand

beach

2 **Ask and answer.**

What can you see at the beach?

I can see sand.

Vocabulary presentation: the world around us

 **1** 🎵🎧 116–117 ▶ **Listen and sing. Do karaoke.**

12

I'm writing a new song,
I'm writing a new song.
At the beach, at the beach.

Suzy's getting a lot of shells,
Suzy's getting a lot of shells.
At the beach, at the beach.

Scott's swimming in the ocean,
Scott's swimming in the ocean.
At the beach, at the beach.

Dad's walking on the sand,
Dad's walking on the sand.
At the beach, at the beach.

Mom's reading in the sun,
Mom's reading in the sun.
At the beach, at the beach …

 2 **Ask and answer.**

What's Sally doing?   She's writing a song.

1 🎧 118 ▶ **Listen and answer.**

Do you want to go to a big city?

Where do you want to go on vacation?

I want to go to the mountains.

2 **Play and say.**

I want to go to the mountains.

I want to go to the mountains, and I want to go to the beach.

Language presentation and practice 1: *Where do you want to go? I want to go to the mountains.*

1  Listen and point. Say the chant.

I want a 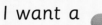,

And you want some .

She wants some ,

And he wants some .

They want a,

And we want a.

She wants a,

And he wants a.

2 120 Listen and say the letter.

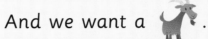 Which melon do you want?

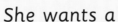 I want the big green one.

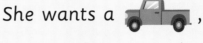 That's *m*.

3 Read and circle.

Sue's on vacation with her **grandma / dad / cousin**. They're **in the mountains / at the beach / in the city**, and it's fun. This morning they're in a shoe store. They're looking at some **boots / shoes / socks** for her vacation. Sue wants the **red / green / blue** ones. It's her favorite color.

They go to a café for lunch. Sue wants **a pie and fries / meatballs and salad / sausages and beans**, and she'd like ice cream, too. She can have chocolate, orange, or banana ice cream. She wants **chocolate / orange / banana**. She loves ice cream!

monty's sounds and spelling

1 🎧 121 ▶ **Watch and say.**

A **p**urple **c**at with a **k**ite in a tr**ee**
And a **ch**icken **p**ainting a **wh**ale.
A **hi**ppo with a **sp**ider on its no**se**
And a **j**ellyfish **pl**a**y**ing with a **sn**ail!

2 **Say and play.**

Is the girl drinking juice?   Yes!

Write it with me!

   __ __ icken, __ __ ale, hi __ __ o, and sn __ __ l!

1 🎧 122 ▶ **Watch the video.**

Marie's geography

Where do you want to explore?

 1 ▶ **Watch and answer.**

2 **What do you need? Look and say.**

In the caves I need …   In the ocean …   In the mountains …

3 🎧 124 **Listen. Check (✓) the boxes.**

 map ☐   🪢 rope ☐   🔦 flashlight ☐   air tank ☐   ⛺ tent ☐

 mask ☐   boots ☐   snorkel ☐   wetsuit ☐   helmet ☐

Fact

Mammoth Cave in the USA is 650 kilometers long. You can choose from 15 different tours.

Project

Plan an adventure.

Trevor's values

Help on vacation

1 **Read and match.**

How can you help on vacation?

a
I'm Ben, and I'm ten. I'm on vacation at an elephant park. It's cool! These elephants don't have a family. We wash them when they are dirty. Here, I'm giving a baby elephant a banana!

I love animals!

Ben

b
I'm Sue. I'm a teacher, and I'm on vacation in the mountains. The mountains are beautiful and green. I'm teaching these children outside!

It's fun. We are very happy!

Sue

c
I'm Grace. I'm on vacation at the beach. The beach is dirty. There are a lot of plastic bottles and cups, and the seabirds can't fly or swim.

I'm picking up trash with my friends and family.

Grace

2 🎧 125 **Listen and say "yes" or "no."**

Grace is on vacation in the mountains.   No.

Review Units 9, 10, 11, and 12

1 🎧 126 Listen and correct.

The boy's wearing a green shirt.

No, he's wearing a red shirt.

2 Look and say with a friend.

In picture one the woman's reading, but in picture two she's writing.

1 Play the game.

Red square – Read and do.
Blue square – What's this?
Green square – What's he/she doing?

Finish

You have your hat. Go forward 2 squares.

You don't have your hat. Go back 2 squares.

Your kite doesn't have a tail. Go back 1 square.

The ocean's dirty. Go back 2 squares.

The ocean's clean. Go forward 2 squares.

Start

Grammar reference

| Who's he? | This is my brother, Scott. He's seven. |
| Who's she? | This is my sister, Suzy. She's four. |

Who's he? = Who is he?   he's = he is   she's = she is

How many desks are there?	There are a lot of desks.
There's a ruler.	There isn't a ruler.
There are a lot of desks.	There aren't a lot of desks.
Is there a whiteboard? Are there ten desks?	Yes, there is. / No, there isn't. Yes, there are. / No, there aren't.

there's = there is   there aren't = there are not

| Whose camera is this? | It's Scott's. |
| Whose books are these? | They're Suzy's. |

It's Scott's. = It's Scott's camera.
They're Suzy's. = They're Suzy's books.

Whose green T-shirt is that? Whose socks are those?	It's mine. They're yours.
Is that dress yours, Suzy? Are those socks yours, Scott?	Yes, it is. / No, it isn't. Yes, they are. / No, they aren't.
Which shoes are Scott's? Which shoes are Sally's?	The gray ones are his. The red ones are hers.

It's mine. = It's my T-shirt.

I'm He's / She's You're / They're / We're	singing.
I'm not	flying.
He's not / She's not / It's not (= He isn't / She isn't / It isn't)	
You're not / We're not / They're not (= You aren't / We aren't / They aren't)	
What are you doing, Suzy? What's Grandpa doing?	

Can I have **some meatballs**, please?	Here you are.

I love **donkeys**.	So do I. / I don't.

Where's **the park**?	It's	behind / in front of **the stores**.
Where are **the apartments**?	They're	behind / in front of **the stores**.
Where's **the school**?	It's	between **the café and the park**.
Where are **the stores**?	They're	between **the café and the park**.

He's / She's They're	wearing blue shorts and white shoes. wearing sunglasses and big hats.	
Do **you** Does **he/she**	**have** a watch?	Yes, I do. / No, I don't. Yes, he/she does. No, he/she doesn't.

don't have = do not have   doesn't have = does not have

I He/She	love / like / don't like loves / likes / doesn't like	swimming. playing Ping-Pong.
Do **you** like **reading**?		Yes, I do. / No, I don't.
Does **he/she** like **reading**?		Yes, he/she does. No, he/she doesn't.

doesn't = does not

Look at me / you / him / her / it / us / them.	
Would you like **a burger**?	Yes, please. I'd love one.
Would you like **some lemonade**?	No, thank you. I'd like **some juice**.

Where do you want **to go** on vacation?	I want **to go to** the mountains.
Do you want **to go to** a big city?	I don't want **to go to** a big city.
Which shoes **do you want**?	I want **the red ones**.

Starters Listening

1 🎧 127 **Listen and write the question word. Choose and color.**

> What?   How old?   What number?

> name questions = blue

> number questions = orange

1
_____ is your
family name?

2
_____
is Lucy's sister?

3
_____ is the name
of Tom's friend?

4
_____
is Alex's house?

2 🎧 128 🐵 **Read the question. Listen and write a name or a number. There are two examples.**

Examples

What is the name of Eva's cousin?   Mark

How old is Eva's cousin?   11

Questions

1 What is Mark's family name?   _____

2 How many paintings does Mark have in his house?   _____

3 Which park does Mark like to go to?   _____ Park

4 What number is Mark's house?   _____

5 What is the name of the donkey?   _____

Starters Listening

1 🎧 129 **Talk about the pictures. Then listen and look. Circle the correct picture.**

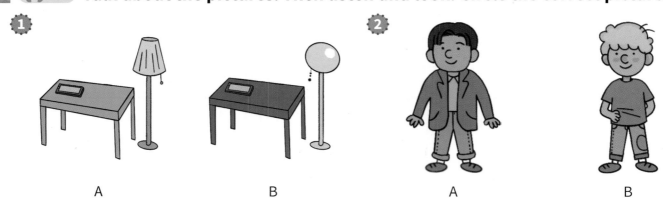

A   B   A   B

2 🎧 130 🐵 **Listen and check (✓) the box. There is one example.**

Which toy is Bill's favorite?

A ☐   B ☐   C ✓

1 What sport is Anna doing this morning?

A ☐   B ☐   C ☐

2 Where is Mrs. Watson's cat?

A ☐   B ☐   C ☐

3 What story is Grace reading?

A ☐   B ☐   C ☐

4 What is Tom eating?

A ☐   B ☐   C ☐

5 Which house is Alex's?

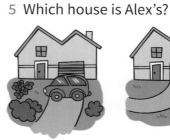  

A ☐   B ☐   C ☐

Starters Reading and Writing

1 Look and read. Draw a line.

This is a T-shirt.   These are shoes.   This is a train.

2 Look and read. Put a ✓ or an ✗ in the box. There are two examples.

Examples

   This is an apple. ✓

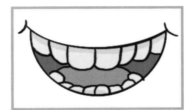   These are feet. ✗

Questions

   This is a skirt. ☐

   These are shoes. ☐

   This is a train. ☐

   This is a boat. ☐

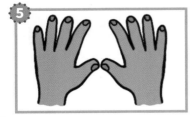   These are hands. ☐

Starters Reading and Writing

1 Read and circle the correct word.

1 Jellyfish live in the **park** / (**ocean**).
2 This monkey has a long **tail** / **nose**.
3 **Lemons** / **Watermelons** are green and red.
4 A **kite** / **cat** is an animal.

2  **Read this. Choose a word from the box. Write the correct word next to numbers 1–5. There is one example.**

Cats

Many people have a cat for a pet. They are nice, beautiful ____animals____ .

Cats live with you in your apartment or (1) _____ . They play with children's toys, for example, small (2) _____ . Cats enjoy sitting next to a window and watching (3) _____ and lizards. In a yard, cats can run, jump on walls, and climb (4) _____ .

Cats love sleeping a lot, too. They sleep in cupboards, under beds, or on a (5) _____ in front of the TV!

Example

animals	trees	armchair	birds

couch	tail	house	balls

Starters Reading and Writing

1 **Look and read. Write "What," "Where," "Who," or "How many."**

_____ are the children?   In a bedroom.

_____ is sitting on the bed?   The girl.

_____ is the girl holding?   A cat.

_____ posters are there?   Two.

2 **Look at the pictures and read the questions. Write one-word answers.**

Examples

Where are the people?   in the ___park___

What animal does the man have?   a ___dog___

Questions

1 What are the children doing?   flying a _____

2 Who is pointing?   the _____

3 Where is the dog?   behind the _____

4 Which animal has the kite?   the _____

5 How many animals are there?   _____

Starters Speaking

1 **Look. Answer the questions with your classmate.**

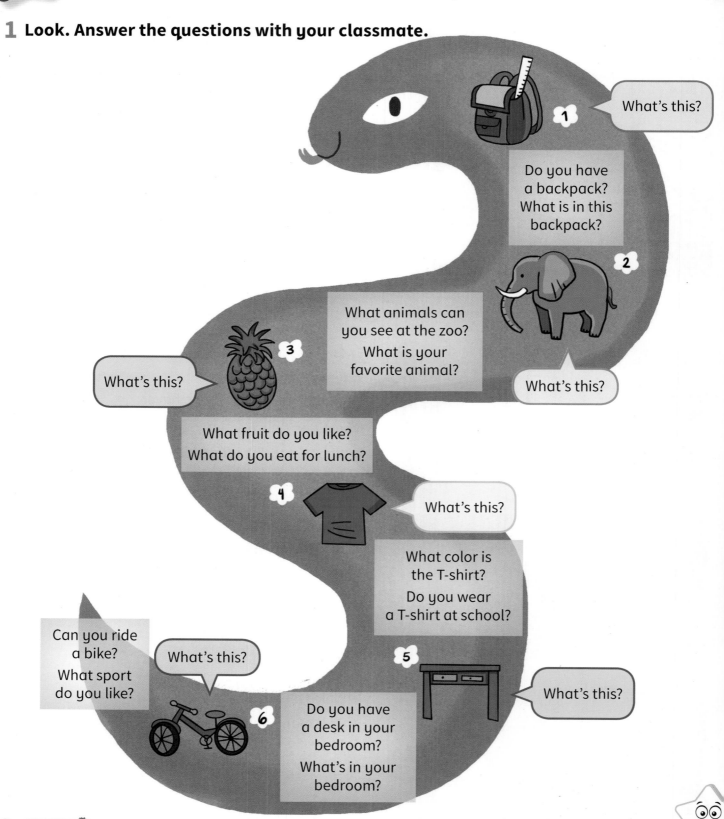

What's this? 1

Do you have a backpack? What is in this backpack?

2 What's this?

What animals can you see at the zoo? What is your favorite animal?

What's this? 3

What fruit do you like? What do you eat for lunch?

4 What's this?

What color is the T-shirt? Do you wear a T-shirt at school?

Can you ride a bike? What sport do you like?

What's this?

5 What's this?

6 Do you have a desk in your bedroom? What's in your bedroom?

2 🎧 131 🐵 **Now look and listen. Answer the questions.**

Starters Speaking

1 🎧 132 **Look and listen. Write one word.**

2 🎧 133 🐵 **Now listen again. Answer the questions.**

> A polar bear.

> An apartment.

Thanks and Acknowledgments

Authors' thanks

Many thanks to everyone at Cambridge University Press & Assessment for their dedication and hard work, and in particular to:

Liane Grainger and Lynn Townsend for supervising the whole project and guiding us calmly through the storms;

Alison Bewsher for her keen editorial eye, enthusiasm and great suggestions;

Amy Few and Liz Wilkie for their hard work, enthusiasm, and good ideas. We would also like to thank all our pupils and colleagues, past, present and future, at Star English academy in Murcia, especially Jim Kelly for his friendship and support throughout the years.

Dedications

For my parents, Eric and Pauline, with much love and gratitude. – CN
For my dearest sisters, Elaine and Teresa. We are Family. – CN
For Shirley and Neville, love – MT
For my great friends in England, who always receive us so kindly, offering their warmth and friendship: Mike and Nicola, and Shaun and Lorraine. – MT

The authors and publishers acknowledge the following sources of copyright material and are grateful for the permissions granted. While every effort has been made, it has not always been possible to identify the sources of all the material used, or to trace all copyright holders. If any omissions are brought to our notice, we will be happy to include the appropriate acknowledgments on reprinting and in the next update to the digital edition, as applicable.

Key: U = Unit

Photography

The following photos are sourced from Getty Images.

U1: Anna Erastova/iStock/Getty Images Plus; **U2:** Science & Society Picture Library/SSPL; Ng Sok Lian/EyeEm; Zocha_K/E+; Thewet Nonthachai/EyeEm; Mosutatsu/E+; Gregor Hofbauer/Moment; Nehru Sulejmanovski/EyeEm; Theerasak Tammachuen/EyeEm; studiocasper/E+; Maria Kovalets/EyeEm; mikroman6/Moment; onebluelight/iStock/Getty Images Plus; Gelpi/iStock/Getty Images Plus; Drazen/E+; Ariel Skelley/Photodisc; monkeybusinessimages/iStock/Getty Images Plus; shironosov/iStock/Getty Images Plus; Indeed; Jose Luis Pelaez Inc/DigitalVision; Anna Erastova/iStock/Getty Images Plus; **U3:** Anna Erastova/iStock/Getty Images Plus; **U4:** EKramar/iStock/Getty Images Plus; Sontaya Panyafu/EyeEm; BRULOVE/iStock/Getty Images Plus; vapadiii/iStock/Getty Images Plus; xmocb/iStock/Getty Images Plus; letty17/E+; hongquang09/iStock/Getty Images Plus; Jose Luis Pelaez Inc/DigitalVision; Rob Lewine; Ariel Skelley/Photodisc; prapassong/iStock/Getty Images Plus; Okea/iStock/Getty Images Plus; studiocasper/E+; ElementalImaging/E+; Bryan Mullennix; Jeffrey Coolidge/DigitalVision; MicroStockHub/iStock/Getty Images Plus; deepblue4you/iStock/Getty Images Plus; Aneduard/iStock/Getty Images Plus; Wladimir Bulgar/Science Photo Library; Image Source; akova/iStock/Getty Images Plus; MirageC/Moment; Hany Rizk/EyeEm; Alex Cao/Photodisc; in4mal/iStock/Getty Images Plus; D3Damon/iStock/Getty Images Plus; Snap Decision/Photographer's Choice RF; popovaphoto/iStock/Getty Images Plus; Westend61; vladru/iStock/Getty Images Plus; StockPlanets/E+; Bombaert Patrick/EyeEm; malerapaso/iStock/Getty Images Plus; Kim Sayer/OJO Images; Wa Nity Canthra/EyeEm; master-garry/iStock/Getty Images Plus; klyaksun/iStock/Getty Images Plus; Anna Erastova/iStock/Getty Images Plus; **U5:** Anna Erastova/iStock/Getty Images Plus; **U6:** Rusty Hill/Photolibrary; SDI Productions/E+; Piotr Krzeslak/iStock/Getty Images Plus; FotografiaBasica/iStock/Getty Images Plus; grau-art/iStock/Getty Images Plus; MAIKA 777/Moment; Kirill Strikha/EyeEm; Shannon M. Lutman/Moment; fcafotodigital/E+; Tom Werner/DigitalVision; Elizabeth Fernandez/Moment; Manuta/iStock/Getty Images Plus; Theerawat Kaiphanlert/Moment; gbh007/iStock/Getty Images Plus; The Picture Pantry/Alloy; Anna Erastova/iStock/Getty Images Plus; **U7:** Anna Erastova/iStock/Getty Images Plus; **U8:** Oleh_Slobodeniuk/E+; Matteo Colombo/DigitalVision; Raimund Koch/The Image Bank; Marco Bottigelli/Moment; Alexander Spatari/Moment; Kinzie Riehm/Image Source; Rebecca Nelson/The Image Bank; Daniel Llaó Calvet/EyeEm; kali9/E+; Todd Warnock/DigitalVision; Gareth Brown/The Image Bank; Nettiya Nithascharukul/EyeEm; Foodcollection; xavierarnau/E+; Pixel_Pig/E+; tbradford/iStock/Getty Images Plus; keiichihiki/E+; Honcha; Olivera Milijic/500px; andras_csontos/iStock/Getty Images Plus; Manuel Breva Colmeiro/Moment; Atanas Mahleliev/500px; Peter Cade/DigitalVision; tsingha25/iStock/Getty Images Plus; swetta/E+; Nancy Nehring/Photodisc; Anna Erastova/iStock/Getty Images Plus; **U9:** Anna Erastova/iStock/Getty Images Plus; **U10:** valda/iStock/Getty Images Plus; RapidEye/iStock/Getty Images Plus; TAPshooter/iStock/Getty Images Plus; valdecasas/iStock/Getty Images Plus; padnpen/iStock/Getty Images Plus; Oksana Struk/iStock/Getty Images Plus; damircudic/E+; A. Witte/C. Mahaney; David Samperio García/EyeEm; Holger Thalmann/Cultura; Rafael Ben-Ari/The Image Bank; Mikael Vaisanen/The Image Bank; mbbirdy/E+; Westend61; PacoRomero/E+; PeopleImages/E+; Image Source; Lorado/E+; Yoshiyoshi Hirokawa/DigitalVision; Marc Dufresne/E+; Anna Erastova/iStock/Getty Images Plus; **U11:** Anna Erastova/iStock/Getty Images Plus; **U12:** Amaia Arozena & Gotzon Iraola/Moment; ColorPlayer/iStock/Getty Images Plus; Christopher Hope-Fitch/Moment; Douglas Klug/Moment; Bonfanti Diego/Cultura; SolStock/E+; ViewStock; Cavan Images; Westend61; LueratSatichob/DigitalVision Vectors; VICTOR/DigitalVision Vectors; TongSur/DigitalVision Vectors; bubaone/DigitalVision Vectors; Levente Bodo/Moment; JGI/Tom Grill; Brett Stevens/Image Source; Antonio Garcia/EyeEm; LauriPatterson/E+; Rob Lewine; Suparat Malipoom/EyeEm; Yoshiyoshi Hirokawa/DigitalVision; hadynyah/E+; PeopleImages/E+; Genicio Zanetti Gz/EyeEm; Suriya Silsaksom/EyeEm; Thomas Barwick/DigitalVision; Roc Canals/Moment; Anna Erastova/iStock/Getty Images Plus;.

The following photos are sourced from another library.

U4: romanklevets/Shutterstock; MasterPhoto/Shutterstock; Aron Brand/Shutterstock; Ingrid Balabanova/Shutterstock; Tanhauzer/Shutterstock; Mikael Damkier/Shutterstock; **U6:** Modernista Magazine/Shutterstock; New Africa/Shutterstock; Cagkan Sayin/Shutterstock **U8:** Phovoir/Shutterstock; LIGHTWORK/Shutterstock.

Illustrations

Blooberry (source Pronk); Beatrice Costamagna, c/o Pickled ink; Chris Jones; Helen Naylor, c/o Plum Pudding; Kelly Kennedy, c/o Sylvie Poggio; Melanie Sharp, c/o Sylvie Poggio; Richard Hoit, Beehive; Xian Xio, c/o Illustration web; Beth Hughes (The Bright Agency); Clara Soriano (The Bright Agency); Dan Crisp (The Bright Agency); Marek Jagucki (Direct artist); Jen Naalchigar (The Bright Agency); Gaby Zermeno (Direct artist); Jake McDonald (The Bright Agency); Matthew Scott (The Bright Agency); Pronk Media Inc.

Cover illustrations by Pronk Media Inc.

Video

Video acknowledgements are in the Teacher Resources on Cambridge One.

Audio

Audio managed by Hyphen Publishing, produced by New York Audio Productions and John Marshall Media.

Songs composed by Robert Lee.

Typeset and design

Blooberry Design

Additional authors

Katy Kelly: Monty's Sounds and Spelling

Rebecca Legros: Marie's math, art, geography, sports, and science

Montse Watkin: Exam folder

Freelance editor

Pippa Mayfield